C000178241

BRITISH RAILWAYS

PAST and PRESENT

COLOUR SPECIAL
First selection

BRITISH RAILWAYS PAST AND PRESENT: It is the summer of 1948, the first months of nationalisation, and snaking around the curves of the original track alignment between Bickley Junction and Petts Wood Junction, south-east London, and approaching the latter, is 'Battle of Britain' 'light Pacific' No 21C154 *Lord Beaverbrook*. The locomotive is still in Southern Railway livery, and will be later renumbered 34054 by BR, and the train is a continental express from Victoria to Dover Marine.

A decade later, in connection with the first phase of the Kent Coast electrification scheme of the late 1950s/early 1960s, this loop was realigned to allow for higher speeds, and was then doubled in 1993 as part of the many line improvements in the area resulting from the advent of the Channel Tunnel. From the same position on 11 December 1993, in the closing months of pre-privatisation British Rail, the 09.08 local service from Victoria to Orpington is formed by Class '466' and Class '465/2' 'Networkers' Nos 466026 leading 465249. *E. R. Wethersett/Brian Morrison*

BRITISH RAILWAYS
PAST and PRESENT

COLOUR SPECIAL
First selection

Past and Present

Past & Present Publishing Ltd

© Past & Present Publishing Ltd

All rights reserved. No part of this publication may be reproduced, stored in a retrieval system or transmitted, in any form or by any means, electronic, mechanical, photocopying, recording or otherwise, without prior permission in writing from Past & Present Publishing Ltd.

First published in May 1994
Reprinted August 1994

The text is adapted from the Introductions to 'British Railways Past and Present' Nos 2, 8, 9, 12, 14, 15, 17 and 20 with additional material by the authors individually credited herein.
The colour material is that added to the same eight volumes in 1994.

British Library Cataloguing in Publication Data

A catalogue record for this book is available from the British Library

ISBN 1 85895 063 5

Past & Present Publishing Ltd
Unit 5
Home Farm Close
Church Street
Wadenhoe
Peterborough PE8 5TE
Tel/fax (0832) 720440

Printed and bound in Great Britain

DIESEL TO ELECTRIC: Brand-new English Electric Type 4 No D205 waits to take the London express from Norwich Thorpe station in 1958. At this time locomotives were still green with the British Railways roundel emblem and no yellow warning panel on the front, railwaymen wore old-style headgear (changed twice since), and schoolboys wore school caps and short trousers.

In 1991 the London Intercity expresses - electrically hauled - arrive and depart from platform 1 on the left, while local trains to Cromer, Yarmouth and Lowestoft use the former London train platforms. It is the swansong of the Class '101' 'Heritage' DMUs - 'Sprinters' and the Regional Railways 'Express' Class 158s are beginning to appear, providing regular cross-country runs as far as Liverpool. *Andrew Ingram/Des Saunders*

'BRITISH RAILWAYS PAST AND PRESENT'

Will Adams

What is it about 'past and presenting' that is so absorbing? What makes grown men set off into the back of beyond armed with only a pruning saw, step-ladders, camera, dog-eared OS map and a 30-year-old railway photograph? How is it that a single modest book published some ten years ago has become a thriving series of 20 volumes - with the likelihood of a further 20 to follow before the entire country is covered?

Certainly no one could have predicted the success of 'British Railways Past and Present' when *No 1: Cumbria* appeared back in 1985. More than 1,700 locations in over 40 counties have so far been sought out and 'past' views replicated by our intrepid authors and photographers.

In some instances they have found a picturesque but archaic steam railway transformed into a modern electric network with clean, quiet trains running at speeds undreamed of in the '50s. Sadly, in perhaps more cases they have found a vital element of our social fabric completely swept away in the name of modernisation and/or political expediency, and now lost for ever under a weed-strewn wilderness, a housing or industrial estate, or supermarket car park. Putting the 'past' and the 'present' side by side, as this series does, allows the reader, even without further authorial comment, to decide what has gone wrong, and what we can learn from it for the future - if it isn't already too late.

Surely it is this 'side by side' treatment that is the key to the fascination. It enables us to be almost in both places - or times - at once. Certainly it is the nearest we shall ever get to a working 'time-machine'! We can see right in front of our eyes either how *little* has changed in three or four decades - or spot the fragment of gatepost or distant telegraph pole that is the only remaining link between 'then' and 'now'.

This special volume celebrates the tenth year of publication of 'British Railways Past and Present', as well as the introduction of colour photography to the series. It not only brings together the first eight colour sections in a single book for the benefit of those regular readers who already have the black & white originals, but will also serve as a 'sampler' for anyone who is new to this most intriguing of publishing success stories.

So to whet your appetite, let's accompany the authors of the first eight 'colour editions' as they describe their chosen areas, and the events that befell them as they attempted to stand with 'one foot in the past'. . .

CORNWALL AND DEVON

David Mitchell

A peninsula largely separated from Devon and the rest of England by the River Tamar, Cornwall is probably the most distinctive county in the country. Its isolation has helped to foster an independent spirit among its inhabitants, not least in the celebration of Celtic traditions and the revival of their own language.

The mining of tin, copper and lead in the county dates from before Roman times, but activity reached a peak in the 18th and 19th centuries when the development of the steam engine and pump enabled workers to go deeper underground. A notable pioneer who did much to develop steam power was Richard Trevithick, who was born in Camborne in 1771. Most of Cornwall's early railways were constructed to carry ore, but their lives were relatively short as cheaper production methods in other countries led to the gradual closure of most mines.

With the opening of the Cornwall Railway in 1859 this isolated land was finally linked to the rest of the country, and the event aided the fishing and farming industries that were now afield. More importantly in the long run, the arrival of the railway encouraged visitors to travel to this land of mystery and legend, with its variety of attractions including both a mild climate and a magnificent coastline.

Most railway development within the Duchy was initiated by local people, but by the turn of the century the Great Western Railway had acquired the majority of the lines and was to dominate the scene thereafter. Although the London & South Western Railway had purchased the Bodmin & Wadebridge in 1846, it was to be almost 50 years before this line was linked to the rest of its system, and the company's influence was accordingly limited to the north of the county.

The railway network was largely complete by the early years of this century, and other than for certain improvements no great changes took place until the 1960s, a decade that was to see the closure of many of Cornwall's stations and much of its track mileage. Three branches were closed prior to the publication of the Beeching Plan, and that report sounded the death knell for most of the others. Fortunately, however, the county fared a little better than certain other parts of British Railways, and the Looe, St Ives and truncated Callington branches were all reprieved. Along with the Newquay and Falmouth branches, they still perform a valuable service to their communities and provide a link to the outside world via the main line and its HST service to London and the north.

Historically the railway has been closely associated with the development of the china clay industry. Although many of the clay lines have now closed, Railfreight activity in Cornwall is currently almost totally dependent on this traffic, and a large tonnage is still carried either for export or to customers in the north. This business has contributed to the survival of the railway in the Duchy and hopefully will continue to do so for many years to come.

However, the future for Cornwall's railway system is presently unclear. InterCity has indicated its desire to electrify the Paddington to Penzance route early in the 21st century, but recently it has been announced that this will be part of one of the first franchises to be offered under the Government's privatisation plans. It remains to be seen how this misconceived programme will proceed, but there has to be a very real fear that at the very least it might result in through trains terminating at Plymouth.

Turning now to Devon, although it is the third largest county in England, its present-day population is only just over one million, thus reflecting its largely rural character with an economy traditionally based on agriculture. Despite this, railways proliferated during the railway building boom just as elsewhere in the country. Small towns were determined to join the ever-growing network, realising that they would soon lose their influence and trade if they did not.

The railway history of the area features the growth of two major companies, the Great Western and the London & South Western, each seeking to spread its influence, even if only to deny the progress of the other! This competition was further complicated by the GWR's choice of the 7-foot 'broad gauge'.

Through its antecedents the GWR was first on the scene and was able to develop a main line through the county with fast and frequent expresses, and fed by branch lines on either side. It also benefited from serving what were generally the wealthier areas, and it helped to enhance this prosperity. In contrast, the later arrival of the LSWR held back the economic development of the areas it served. In particular its network of lines west of Exeter, the so-called 'Withered Arm', did not warrant or indeed receive the level of service enjoyed to the south.

Despite this, only two ex-LSWR passenger lines (the narrow-gauge Lynton & Barnstaple, and the Turnchapel branch) had closed prior to the publication of the Beeching report in 1963, whereas half of Devon's former GWR branches had passed into oblivion by then. Subsequently, though, the former LSWR routes were to be decimated, as can be seen from the photographs in the book.

As an enthusiast it is easy to over-sentimentalise the closure of any railway, and it has to be admitted that some routes had probably outlasted their value. Although not a typical example, it is arguable that the ND&CJLR (Torrington to Halwill) line was an anachronism when it opened in 1925, and its survival as a passenger line for 40 years must rate as something of a miracle, or a reflection upon a remote management lacking in financial acumen. Possibly if earlier attempts had been made at cost-cutting and modernisation, the wholesale closures of the 1950s and 1960s might have been partly avoided.

When it came, the dieselisation of the South West was a quick process as the area was earmarked by BR's Western Region authorities for the early eradication of steam. This led to the short-lived diesel-hydraulic era, now also a part of history, but a fascinating period in itself, and I was pleased to be able to include a number of rare views in the book.

Today it is gratifying to report that the former GWR main line is thriving with frequent and well-patronised services to London, the Midlands and the North. As elsewhere, the coming of the HST captured the public's imagination and currently the fastest train of the day allows a journey from Exeter to London in only 2 hours 4 minutes.

LISKEARD, CORNWALL: On an overcast (and damp, judging by the open umbrella) 11 July 1959, 4-6-0 No 1023 *County of Oxford* arrives with the 12.5 pm Plymouth to Truro stopper. The up platform is crowded with passengers awaiting their train, which is also signalled. The track running off to the left beyond the platform leads to the station and yard serving the Looe branch.

Although the down platform buildings have been demolished and replaced by a nondescript shelter, the branch to Looe survives, as does the signal box in this 5 April 1992 view of the first pocket of surviving semaphore signals on the journey west from Paddington! Class '20' Nos 20901 and 20904 arrive from Plymouth with the Chipman's weed control train. *Peter W. Gray/David Mitchell*

No passenger routes have closed since the Kingswear line was sold in 1972, whilst stations have reopened - the success of Tiverton Parkway is a hopeful indication for the future. At the time of writing there is a suggestion that the Bere Alston to Tavistock line could be reopened as part of Plymouth's plans to overcome congestion.

After years as a 'Cinderella' route, the ex-LSWR main line has undergone something of a revival, and Exeter Central is now the western outpost of Network SouthEast. Unfortunately the once hoped for extension of the third rail does not now look likely, and the increasingly unreliable Class '50s' were replaced by Class '159' 'Sprinters' in 1992.

Freight tonnage has never been particularly high in this area and the viability of present Railfreight operations is largely dependent on clay traffic, some of which originates in Devon but the majority of which passes through en route from the main producing areas in Cornwall. There is, however, an interesting variety of traffic, some of which was recorded in this volume, but the demise of Speedlink operations is a cause for concern.

It is to be hoped that the growing environmental lobby will encourage the Government to develop a more enlightened view on railway matters in the South West, and that any future similar book will be able to report on an expanding rather than a contracting system.

I was growing up in St Austell during the period when most of the 'past' photographs were taken. They not only record scenes that I missed, partly through youthful ignorance, but have also helped me to relive those distant but lingering memories - St Blazey and the first ever shed-bash; watching the Fowey 'auto' at Golant one evening; cabbing No 41320 at Bodmin North; crossing the Royal Albert Bridge behind a 'Hall' and looking down at the Tamar below. . .

When I came to take to 'present' photographs, my abiding memories concern the weather. The Devon photos were mainly taken during the glorious summer of 1990, when perhaps the greatest problem was waiting for the dull day that certain shots required. During a week's holiday in July, the threat of sunstroke was the main concern!

In contrast, many expeditions to Cornwall in 1992 were affected by poor weather. In particular my plans during a six-day session in August of that year were upset when 2½ days were wasted by heavy rain.

Finding the locations did not generally prove to be too much of a problem, either from my own knowledge or with the help of the products of the Ordnance Survey, both past and present. However, several spots, particularly where the railway site has been obliterated, did require much exploration looking for any surviving features in the hope of obtaining a reasonably accurate equivalent view.

On occasions a decision had to be made as to whether an exact replica view was to be obtained, although this might result in a close-up of a bush. . . Alternatively, should a slightly different angle be used to provide a more interesting present scene? My inclination is generally to go for the latter, and most comments that I have received support this view. However, one or two purists have criticised it. . .

One aspect that has to be accepted is that the 'present' does not stand still. I revisited Chacewater several months after my initial session when I learned that some track had been removed; the BR scene is an ever-changing one (and perhaps the privatised one will be even more so), and a present view could itself soon be obsolete. If nothing else this might provide an impetus for a second series of books in due course!

My aim where BR was still operating was to portray as much variety of motive power, etc, as possible, and this was not always too easy with today's standardised railway. Photographing irregular freight workings can cause problems; three visits had to be made to both Heathfield and Truro, for example, before the desired views could be obtained.

It was sometimes necessary to be provided with some basic gardening equipment, and of course the standard issue railway photographer's step-ladder, so that battle could be waged with the undergrowth and other obstructions at certain locations, for example Chilsworthy; but the only other problem that I can recall was the herd of cows that disturbed me in the field at Loddiswell.

My abiding memory is the generally very friendly welcome I received from the occupants of former stations. Even if they were not railway enthusiasts they nearly always seemed to take an interest in the former use of their property, and were keen to see the photos I had with me, as well as showing me items that they had collected over the years.

Perhaps the highlight for me was the young lady at one such station who hurried indoors to cover herself up, when my approach up a long drive interrupted her topless sunbathing session!

KENT AND EAST SUSSEX

Brian Morrison & Brian Beer

We now move to the opposite end of the South Coast, subject of the 20th volume of the 'British Railways Past and Present' series. Where once 'Schools', 'Battle of Britain', Maunsell 'Mogul' and Wainwright 'C' Class 0-6-0 locomotives proliferated, along with a variety of bone-shaking electric multiple units of varying vintage, the railways of Kent and the eastern parts of Sussex are now thought by many to consist solely of electric trains from London to the coastal towns, and of similarly operated suburban services. Certainly these trains are of considerable importance, but the lines within this south-eastern part of the United Kingdom remain quite complex, and include cross-country services, a considerable amount of freight, some remaining branch lines - and the Channel Tunnel trains yet to come, although a few precursors in this respect were able to be included in the book, published in the spring of 1994.

Present-day views of photographs taken years before vary considerably. Apart from the motive power, some locations have seen very little change, whereas others are unrecognisable. Generally speaking the main lines remain, but a number of the branches have gone, and others are now in the welcome

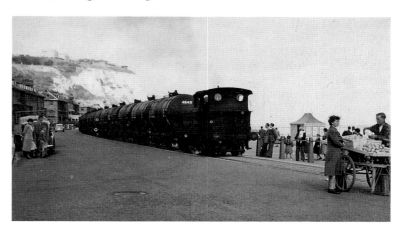

ALONG THE PROM: On 7 September 1950 diminutive Wainwright Class 'P' 0-6-0T No 31558 passes slowly along Dover Promenade, Kent, with a haul of Shell wagons, probably containing marine fuel for the harbour craft.

Today the track alongside the road has long been removed, and parked cars occupy the same position. No longer can a barrow-boy sell his wares from the middle of the road, and although the cliff and clifftop buildings are still apparent, a mass of apartment blocks now stands where the seaside residences once advertised 'Bed and Breakfast'. *S. J. Reerdon/Brian Beer*

hands of preservationists. It is no longer possible to travel by rail to Gravesend West, Westerham, Tunbridge Wells West, Hawkhurst, All Hallows, Lydd, Hythe, Bexhill West, Kemp Town, or on the Cuckoo Line, but the Kent & East Sussex Railway remains within the bounds of this volume, as does the southern portion of the Bluebell Line at Sheffield Park, the East Kent Railway, and the Lavender Line, truncated at Uckfield, but still in existence around Isfield.

The Westerham branch provided a couple of challenges. In locating Brasted station, comparison of old and new Ordnance Survey maps showed that the scene of the branch train in 1961 was taken from what is now the hard shoulder of a section of the M25 motorway! A very quick stop, a very quick photograph of passing vehicles, and a very quick departure were called for. . .

The branch terminus itself had vanished completely beneath modern warehouses. It was clear from maps where the station had been, but the standpoint of the 'past' photograph was not apparent. An elderly gentleman on an early Sunday morning stroll passed by, and upon enquiring from him if he was aware of the exact position from which the old view had been taken, he smiled and informed us that he had lived in one of the cottages shown in the print for the past 40 years, and what is more his uncle had been the Station Master. Needless to say, the angle of our copy shot is exact.

One has to seize one's chances when one can to capture just the right shot. Currently only one train a day traverses the line to Dungeness, the Thursdays-only nuclear flask from Sellafield; then one Saturday an engineer's train was scheduled to go down the line. We arrived at the location of the 'past' view of Brookland Halt very early on a dull and drizzly morning, and had just thought about pouring a coffee from the flask when the unmistakeable sound of a 'Crompton' was heard. The train was running at least three-quarters of an hour early! A mad dash to approximately the same spot as the old photo (which luckily turned out to be correct), an exposure of 1/250sec at f2, and the result is in the book. Maybe not the best, but better than having to take a weekday off to make the trip again in another five days' time.

Another 'last chance' episode was at Uckfield, where the old station was pho-

tographed from the footbridge. A few weeks after we took the equivalent view the bridge was completely dismantled, and exact copies would now be impossible.

Nearly all of the various 'Southern' engine sheds in the area have disappeared, although remains of some can still be seen. Just two, Slade Green and Ramsgate, survive to attend to the needs of modern traction, and these are now known as traction depots. Tunbridge Wells West still survives to serve the future needs of the Tunbridge Wells & Eridge Railway Preservation Society, and the old repair shops building at St Leonards also houses preserved motive power of more modern variety. The two works complexes within the boundaries of this book are Ashford and Brighton; most of the Ashford buildings remain in use in one way or another, but the Brighton site is now a large car park. The look on the face of a passer-by as I paced out the position from which the 'past' interior photograph had been taken inside Brighton Works, using a drawing, then proceeded to take what appeared to be a photograph of two random parked cars, was a sight to behold!

To give the reader some idea of the hardships endured in the course of compiling a 'Past and Present' book, we could cite the example of Eastbourne shed. The old shed buildings were some way from the station, and access to the grassed-over site could only be found through a gap in the base of a tall wire fence, through which one had to slide feet first. Immediately on the other side of the hole was a short but fairly steep embankment which it was quite easy to slide down. After taking the present view, however, I [BM] realised that it was not possible to return through the hole, uphill and in a head-first direction, without continually slithering down the slope. What I really needed was some assistance, but my co-author was blissfully sitting in his car listening to the radio, and no amount of shouting could attract his attention! Eventually I managed to struggle back through the hole, but had to leave the camera bag behind and return for it after I had explained the problem. Despite the state of my shoes and trousers, he still thought it was funny.

At the site of Newhaven Swing Bridge only the old iron gate to the bridge still exists, the area now being something of a wasteland perimeter to a lorry park. In positioning for the copy photograph, the local rat population was disturbed, and on a number of occasions one would scamper across the old gateway. We tried to catch one on film in order to emulate a Terence Cuneo painting, but failed!

You can see the trouble to which one must go to obtain accurate present-day views, and in most cases the modern view is fairly exact, with feet planted firmly in the same position as dictated by the photographer from years past. In a few locations, however, elevation has gone, and in a few other instances the foliage forced a slightly different angle to be taken, or in some instances resulted in the quest having to be aborted altogether.

OXFORDSHIRE

Laurence Waters & Tony Doyle

The Great Western Railway first entered Oxfordshire in June 1840 when the Reading to Steventon section of Brunel's main line from London to Bristol bisected the county boundary to the east of Goring. The City of Oxford was connected to the rail network in June 1844 with the opening by the Oxford Railway Company of a 9½-mile branch from Didcot Junction. Prior to this passengers from Oxford had to travel south and use the station at Steventon. The construction of the Oxford Railway and its subsequent extension through to Birmingham in 1852 gave the Great Western, and Brunel in particular, a Broad Gauge foothold in the Midlands. In fact, we have perhaps the ultimate past and present combination in the book - an 1852 engraving of the original station at Oxford contrasted with streets of 1870s/1880s terraced housing that occupies the site today, 140 years on!

By the turn of the century the railway map in the county was almost complete, with very few Oxfordshire towns and villages more than a few miles from a station. And by then it was not just the Great Western that dominated the county because the London & North Western Railway had its own lines serving both Oxford and Banbury.

The growth of lines in Oxfordshire essentially came to an end in April 1910 with the completion by the Great Western of the 18¼-mile Ashendon Junction at Aynho section of the Paddington to Birmingham 'cut off' route.

A general increase in passenger traffic between the two wars saw the Great Western open several new passenger Halts in the county, and during the Second World War the railway network was expanded once again with new goods yards being opened at Yarnton, Banbury, Hinksey and Moreton (Didcot). The resulting increase in traffic both during and after the war meant that Oxford became an operating bottleneck, a situation that continued for many years.

During the 1950s the county saw its first branch line closures with Faringdon, Woodstock, Wallingford and Watlington all losing their passenger services. By 1963 they had been joined by Chipping Norton, Thame, Fairford and Abingdon.

Steam traction came to an end in the county during September 1966. The very last official Western Region steam working had taken place several months earlier when, on 3 January 1966, No 6998 *Burton Agnes Hall* pulled the 2.20 pm service from Bournemouth to York between Oxford and Banbury.

It is interesting to reflect that in 1950 there were 64 stations open in Oxfordshire, while today there are just 22. For such a small county Oxford was blessed with a wide variety of lines and although many of these are now closed the area still continues to provide many interesting locations for the railway photographer.

One in particular sticks in my mind. This was one of the closed stations, and the only access was up an embankment. Wet weather had left the bank slippery, but I struggled to the top holding a camera in one hand and the 'past' photo in the other. Fighting my way through the undergrowth at the top, I walked straight off the platform which, unbeknown to me, was still in situ under a considerable growth of wild roses. I was stuck, and it took me over 10 minutes to extract myself to take the photo. On leaving the site I fell down the embankment, and left covered in mud and rose thorns - but with the shot in the bag!

In 1974 new boundary changes saw Didcot and much of the Vale of the White Horse, previously in Berkshire, absorbed into Oxfordshire. Therefore, in order to make matters simple and the book more interesting, we decided to use the 'new' Oxfordshire as our

PASSING TRAINS: On 12 September 1958 a pair of 'Modified Halls' pass at Kings Sutton, south of Banbury. In the foreground is No 7901 *Fountain Hall* on a down goods, and speeding through the station is an up goods behind No 7911 *Lady Margaret Hall*.

The scene in 1994 shows 'Chiltern Line' 'Turbo' No 165029 departing with a morning service to Marylebone. The sidings and yard - and the 'mechanical horse' on the right - are all things of the past. *Author's collection/P. Heath*

boundary line. This enabled us to include many of these locations, to the south of Oxford, that would have otherwise been excluded.

In selecting the pictures we resisted the temptation to include a train in every shot. We both feel that, certainly at some locations, the inclusion of a train often obscures much of the interesting detail that was once there and has now gone. Moreover, such is the pace of change in motive power matters that the train can serve to turn a 'present' shot into a 'past' one quite soon; several photographs show Network SouthEast loco-hauled services between Oxford and Paddington, but since June 1992 all have been replaced by the new Network Class '165' Turbo units.

Producing the book was certainly great fun, albeit tinged with a certain amount of sadness, travelling around the county revisiting many of those long gone lines and stations.

EAST ANGLIA

Des Saunders & Richard Adderson

Geographically and historically there have been many widely varied definitions of East Anglia - some 'regional' media would include Northampton and Corby within its boundaries. From a railway point of view, the area can reasonably be described as that served by the former Great Eastern Railway, with the obvious exception of the London suburban lines, thus taking in all of Norfolk and Suffolk, most of Essex and parts of Cambridgeshire.

Quite where suburbia ends and East Anglia begins is open to debate, and probably varies as London's influence spreads ever wider to take in what were once undoubtedly provincial areas. We had to start somewhere, so we drew an imaginary east-west line through Southminster, Chelmsford and Harlow; south of this line was 'London', while northward lay the 'East Anglia' that is covered in the book.

First we dealt with what is now the 'West Anglia' main line of Network SouthEast to Kings Lynn, and also looked at some lines in the west of the area that did not survive to the

days of red lamp-posts. Reaching the North Norfolk coast at Hunstanton, we returned again to 'Outer Suburbia', to the lines through Colchester to Clacton, Harwich and Ipswich. Getting away from commuterland, we then looked at the fascinating network of rural lines on the Essex/Suffolk/Cambridgeshire borders, before continuing northwards along the East Suffolk line and the main line to Norwich.

Our tour of Norfolk revealed that the county, being essentially a rural area, has suffered more than most in the way of railway closures, but at the time of writing the surviving lines appeared to have a secure future.

With all due respect to the Southwold, Mid Suffolk and Colne Valley & Halstead railways, it was only in Norfolk that the GER had any real competition. This was in the form of the Midland & Great Northern Joint Railway, which ran from Yarmouth across the county to Kings Lynn and ultimately on to Peterborough and the Midlands. Formed in 1893 by the amalgamation of a number of locally promoted lines, the 'Joint', as it became known, handled heavy traffic over largely single track in its heyday. With the exception of a few freight spurs, though, the 'Joint's' 182 route miles were closed completely on 28 February 1959 - perhaps the first major railway closure in the country, and long before the infamous Dr Beeching appeared on the scene.

In the '50s and '60s, when the majority of the 'past' photographs in the book were taken, there was of course considerable variety in the railway scene, and it was this variety that was the attraction to many enthusiasts of the era. With trains likely to be formed of a rich selection of rolling-stock anything up to 40 years old, and to be hauled by any one of a number of locomotive classes, there was a sense of anticipation to see what would actually turn up. On the other hand, there was an air of permanence about the stations, where in many cases ancient lamps and signs dating back to pre-Grouping days lasted well into the 1950s.

By and large it is the opposite that applies today, as there is an unprecedented degree of uniformity and predictability in the trains themselves. To us, while visiting locations for the book, the uncertainty and anticipation was not about the type of train we would see, but more about how things might have

CHANGE FOR FRAMLINGHAM: In April 1965, just before the Framlingham branch was finally closed, D5045 curves away from the main Ipswich-Yarmouth line at Wickham Market Junction, Suffolk, with a light-weight goods train for the branch.

By the spring of 1991 the trackbed and cutting sides of the branch were rapidly disappearing under the vegetation, but the crossing-keeper's cottage can still just be made out through the trees. This section of the East Suffolk line has now been singled, but the sleeper-built ballast bin has survived the changes of a quarter of a century. A three-car Class '101' DMU heads for Ipswich.
H. N. James/Richard Adderson

changed. Would it be possible to find a similar viewpoint to yesteryear? Would any of yester-year's features still be there, or would the 'bus-shelter'-type buildings and overhead catenary have removed all traces? In many cases, of course, we knew we would not see any trains, and here the question was even more basic - would there be anything to see there at all, or would a road improvement scheme or industrial estate have obliterated

the site entirely? But when we were able to find features to link the photographs, whether obvious or not, the sense of satisfaction for both of us was no less than it would have been if, in the old days, a 'J15' and two ancient coaches had appeared instead of the expected diesel railcar.

Such was the local interest in the book that in spring of 1992 an interview was arranged with the local independent TV station, to take place at the site of the old Norwich Victoria station. I was ready to discuss with the interviewer how the book came about, how Richard Adderson and I came in contact, how the pictures were gathered, and tales of our expeditions across East Anglia in search of today's photographs. However, to my dismay he began to ask me about the postwar decline of railways, to me a rather threadbare subject; I was completely thrown for a moment or two, and it shows on the videotape! In the end all went well, however, and I quite enjoyed this new experience.

During the course of the interview a group of schoolchildren on their way home along an adjacent footpath called over 'Can we be on the television, mister?' 'All right,' replied the interviewer. The cameras were waved around and the youngsters trotted happily home.

In a project of this sort there are two main enemies, nature and man. We think that East Anglia can lay claim to as many, if not more, closed railway lines than any other part of the country, and consequently this book perhaps more than others in the series has a great proportion of 'shock' comparisons, which is where nature and man come into the picture. There are some locations where it is impossible to reach the same spot short of having a machete or bulldozer.

Our first photographic trip to Lavenham in the summer of 1991, just 30 years after the station closed, proved how difficult it could be to match the shots. When the prints were received, close inspection of the size and growth of the trees convinced us that we had chosen the wrong spot. There was another road bridge some 500 yards further back, so a week or so later we retraced our steps and took another photograph, this time from the correct bridge. Would anyone like a photograph of a dense wood from a road bridge somewhere near Lavenham?

The tell-tale remains of railways are everywhere in East Anglia, to your left and right -

the line of post-and-wire fencing for no apparent reason enclosing a line of scrubland crossing the road where a small gatekeeper's cottage remains, once the basic accommodation for a man and wife on duty, sometimes round the clock.

We found that the production of an old photograph was a key that opened many doors; the vast majority of owner-occupiers were only too happy to show us around, point out remaining memorabilia, and show, in their opinion, the exact spot where the previous photograph was taken. Present-day railwaymen for the most part were also very interested, the older men particularly wallowing in nostalgia.

The welcome was sometimes rather guarded, however. While taking photographs at the old Lenwade station a very unfriendly alsatian accompanied me for some 300 yards along the trackbed barking loudly and separated from me by only what appeared to be a rather flimsy barbed wire fence. I was hoping that it would hold. The dog obviously thought otherwise. . .

SOUTH AND WEST YORKSHIRE

John S. Whiteley & Gavin Morrison

This was only the second book in the series, first published back in 1986, before some of the region's lines came 'under the wires' and other modern developments of the 1990s took place. It is introduced first by John Whiteley.

Dr Beeching has much to answer for - a sentiment which I am sure is shared by many railway enthusiasts. Certainly he was responsible for closing a considerable number of lines, which at that time were considered uneconomic, in both South and West Yorkshire, and of all the lines proposed for closure at that period, former GNR suburban lines fared worse than most. Generally this was because the GNR lines had duplicated the earlier and less heavily engineered routes.

While none can deny that there was probably more duplication of lines in South and West Yorkshire than there was in other parts of the country, and indeed many towns were served by at least two rival main-line pre-Grouping companies, some lines which could have served a very useful purpose in the years to come were lost for ever. As our roads become more and more choked under the sheer volume of traffic, it is now becoming generally accepted that some of these lines, which were declared uneconomic by Dr Beeching, would have had a role to play in today's transport system.

In fact, it is somewhat ironic that very recently several new stations have been opened in suburban areas in an attempt to alleviate the traffic problems on our already congested roads. It is also possible that had certain lines survived for a few more years beyond the Beeching era, they would now have become major tourist attractions. One line which immediately comes to mind in this respect is the extension from Ilkley to Skipton via Bolton Abbey. How pleasant it would be today to see a preserved steam locomotive pottering through this section of the picturesque Yorkshire Dales.

My first recollection of railways in what was then the West Riding of Yorkshire was the line from Bradford Exchange to Halifax and on into Lancashire. I attended Junior School at Lightcliffe until the age of 11, and the School was prominently situated overlooking the station and the adjacent goods yard. Passengers workings at that time were generally in the hands of Stanier Class '5' 4-6-0s and 2-6-4 tanks, and the goods yard was often shunted by Aspinall 0-6-0s. It is hard to believe that in the 1950s between Bradford and Halifax alone there were stations at Low Moor, Lightcliffe and Hipperholme. The station at Lightcliffe closed in 1965 and the goods yard has now been buried beneath modern housing.

After leaving school I worked for a time in Dewsbury, the office being only a stone's throw away from Dewsbury Central station, which was on the GNR line from Bradford to Wakefield. At one time this was part of the dense network of Great Northern suburban routes in the textile district, and at lunchtime I used to enjoy seeing 'N1' 0-6-2Ts or 'J50' 0-6-0Ts tackling the climb to either Batley or Earlsheaton. Dewsbury Central station was allowed to decay for several years after closure, but it has now disappeared during the construction of a new ring road and it is difficult to even find the trackbed in places between Dewsbury and Wakefield.

One of my fondest memories of steam in the West Riding was the cramped terminus at Leeds Central, which often reverberated to the Kylchap exhausts of Gresley, Thompson and Peppercorn 'Pacifics'. From Leeds Central there was a steep climb, past Holbeck High Level and Copley Hill motive power depot, which extracted every ounce of power from the locomotive, be it on a local working or a heavy express bound for King's Cross. I well remember looking forward to my half-day release from the office to Technical College, while I was studying for professional examinations, as unknown to my employers this allowed me an occasional opportunity to have a morning on the lineside at Leeds, which I found far more rewarding than studying! It was hard to image in those days that Leeds Central would soon be but a memory, and today all trace of the station and most of the line to Copley Hill has disappeared as a result of the relentless march of redevelopment.

The former LNWR main line between Leeds and Huddersfield passes through Dewsbury, and this provided me with an opportunity to see Edge Hill 4-6-0s in the shape of 'Royal Scots', 'Patriots' and 'Jubilees'. This route still sees a considerable amount of InterCity traffic, which back in 1986 when the book was being prepared were hauled almost exclusively by Class '45/1s' and Class '47s', themselves now part of the past on this route.

Not far from Dewsbury is the Calder Valley main line which, although it did not produce the glamorous motive power of the nearby LNWR route, did produce a constant procession of coal trains from Healy Mills to Lancashire, invariably hauled by either '8F' or 'Austerity' 2-8-0s. For several years during the 1970s and early 1980s a considerable amount of freight traffic was routed to Lancashire via Standedge, but following the reopening of the Calder Valley route after the disastrous fire in Summit Tunnel, this route once again sees a considerable amount of freight traffic, mainly in the shape of oil trains and merry-go-round coal trains. Most of the oil traffic is generated at Stanlow and the MGRs help to feed Fiddlers Ferry power station. Class '47s' and Class '56s' have now taken the place of the 2-8-0s, but at least the railway survives and is still hard at work.

Past and Present Colour

Cornwall

SALTASH was at one time the busiest passenger station in the Duchy. From July 1904 an intensive service of steam rail motor units ran between here and Plymouth and a number of new halts were opened in the area. The up platform was extended in 1908, when other improvements included the erection of a footbridge. Auto-trains were subsequently introduced and in the 1930s a suburban service of almost 50 trains ran each weekday. On 2 January 1960 0-6-0PT No 6419 prepares to leave with the three trailers forming the 3.00 pm departure to Plymouth.

Regular steam working finished in June 1961, and the opening of the Tamar road bridge that year was to bring about a decline in the service. Saltash station is now unmanned, and, as recorded on New Year's Eve 1993, the footbridge and kiosk have disappeared, while the main station building is fenced off and in commercial use. *Peter W. Gray/David Mitchell*

WEARDE signal box, just south-west of Saltash, is pictured on Saturday 25 July 1959 as 4-6-0 No 4976 *Warfield Hall* passes with the 7.50 am Newquay to Manchester train. This view is taken from a road overbridge with the camera pointing in the opposite direction to the picture of Defiance Platform on page 11 of 'BR Past and Present' No 17. The end of the down goods loop can be noted; this ran from a point just beyond Coombe-by-St Stephen viaduct. The water column was used by locomotives standing in the loop.

Apart from the main running lines, all the other items of railway interest have been swept away with only the base of the hut otherwise linking these scenes. HST Power Cars Nos 43142 and 43164 sweep by forming the 8.40 Penzance-Paddington on Sunday 26 September 1993. *Peter W. Gray/David Mitchell*

BODMIN ROAD: 'County' Class 4-6-0 No 1002 *County of Berks* arrives at the station on Whit Monday 18 May 1959 with the down 'Cornishman'. The up starting signal was located on the down platform, and can be seen behind the first coach. The Bodmin branch platform is on the left, the gantry crossing the two tracks forming part of an unusual water tower.

The up platform has been extended and the tracks on the left no longer connect to the main line, although a head-shunt allows Bodmin & Wenford Railway engines to run round; the only rail link with BR is at the other end of the station. The signal box has closed and is now used as a cafe. On 16 January 1994 No 150221 departs on the 13.15 Penzance-Plymouth. *Michael Mensing/David Mitchell*

PENHARGARD: One feature of the fascinating and historic Bodmin & Wadebridge Railway was this water tank in Pencarrow Woods, which was fed by gravity from a passing stream. All trains to Wenfordbridge stopped here as neither the ex-GWR pannier tanks nor their predecessors, the LSWR Beattie well tanks, had sufficient water capacity to complete their journey. Collett 0-6-0PT No 1369 was photographed receiving supplies on 27 April 1963 while working the RCTS/PRC 'Camel Valleyman' special.

The stream still runs down the hillside and beneath the trackbed at this point on its way to join the River Camel, but as seen on 28 December 1993 unfortunately both the water tank and rails have disappeared. However, the local road system is narrow and unsuited to heavy traffic, and there are proposals for the reinstatement of the railway.
Peter W. Gray/David Mitchell

PAR was recorded for posterity at 1.20 pm on Saturday 29 August 1959 as 4-6-0 No 4906 *Bradfield Hall* and 2-6-0 No 5376 arrived with the 12.30 pm Newquay to Paddington train. The station is seen to advantage from this angle with the goods shed prominent in the background.

Although the view today is basically similar, many of the items visible in the past scene have been removed; in particular the up platform is rather bare following the demolition of the main building and removal of the water column. However, a starter signal has been added on the branch side. Passing over the up main on 16 January 1994 are Class '37s' Nos 37670 and 37673 on the 10.05 Burngullow-Irvine. This is currently a thrice-weekly service conveying china clay slurry for the Caledonian Paper Co. *Peter W. Gray/David Mitchell*

BUGLE: After arriving from St Dennis Junction, the Plymouth Railway Circle's 'Cornwall Mineral' special of 28 April 1962 has reversed direction, and 2-6-2Ts Nos 5531 and 4564 are propelling the train for a visit to Carbis Wharf. The Wheal Rose branch trails away in the foreground while the track on the right of the train is the Newquay line, the track from Goonbarrow Junction having been doubled to here in July 1930.

Most of the track visible above was taken out of use in November 1964, with the Carbis branch seeing its last train in 1989. Only the former up 'main' line remains and Class '153' No 153380 is pictured on 28 December 1993 just after it has departed from Bugle station forming the 13.42 Par to Newquay service. *Peter W. Gray/David Mitchell*

PENMERE PLATFORM was opened on 1 June 1925 to serve a growing community to the west of Falmouth. On Whit Monday, 18 May 1959, 2-6-2T No 5537 calls at the halt at the head of the 9.05 am Truro to Falmouth train. When building this branch the Cornwall Railway allowed for future doubling of the track, but this optimism was not to be realised. The track visible to the left of the engine forms part of a loop installed in 1940, together with sidings for an MOD oil depot.

The loop and sidings were taken out of use in 1967. On 28 December 1993 'Heritage' DMU No 117305 is about to leave on the 12.40 Truro-Falmouth. This unit was painted in chocolate and cream livery as part of the 'GW150' celebrations. Although the platform is almost deserted, it is pleasing to report that a goodly number of passengers had just left the train. *Michael Mensing/David Mitchell*

CARBIS BAY: Some idea of the spectacular views that can be obtained on the St Ives branch is apparent in this scene on 9 September 1961 as 2-6-2T No 4564 heads away from Carbis Bay with an ECS working. That date marked the official end of steam working on the line and this locomotive was the last to be serviced at St Ives's little engine shed.

Happily it is still possible for the traveller to enjoy the scenery today, although a diesel unit will provide the transportation. For a spell the Class '142' 'Skippers' were used, as in this July 1986 view, but due to a number of technical defects their stay was a short-lived one. *Both Peter Gray*

SIDMOUTH JUNCTION: On 10 August 1963 Ivatt Class '2' 2-6-2T No 41307 and BR Standard Class '4' 2-6-4T No 80042 curve away from the station and the South Western main line with the 11.45 am Waterloo to Exmouth/Sidmouth service; the 12-coach formation will be split into two portions at Tipton St Johns.

Today the branch formation is still discernible, if very overgrown, but behind the camera the former cutting has been filled in, the land now being part of a field. The main line is partially obscured, but on 3 January 1994 Class '159' 'Sprinter' No 159013 can be seen just after departure from Feniton station (the original name of Sidmouth Junction, and to which it has reverted since reopening in 1971) as the 13.30 Exeter St Davids-Honiton service. Locomotive-hauled trains between Waterloo and Exeter ceased in July 1993, and the 'Sprinters' now provide the service. *Peter W. Gray/David Mitchell*

LYMPSTONE is the first station out of Exmouth on the former LSWR branch from Exmouth Junction. It is seen here from the north as Standard Class '4' 2-6-4T No 80038 departs with the 5.45 pm Exmouth to Exeter train on 7 July 1963. A goods loop had existed to the left of the train, with a short siding leading to a cattle dock. However, the yard closed in April 1960, with the track being removed in September 1962 when the platform-mounted signal box also closed.

The station buildings were demolished in December 1976 and a small shelter now provides the only accommodation. Looking back to 1987 when Class '142' 'Skippers' provided the branch services, No 142022 departs with an Exmouth to Exeter train on 27 September. *Both Peter W. Gray*

UFFCULME: Turning now to former Great Western lines in the county, we first visit the Culm Valley Light Railway, which opened on 29 May 1876 and ran from Tiverton Junction for some $7^1/_2$ miles through picturesque farming country. The route followed closely the course of the River Culm, which enabled construction costs to be kept to a minimum, but the lightly laid and sharply curving track limited the size of both the engines and the stock that could be used. On 15 September 1962 0-4-2T No 1451 leads its ex-Barry Railway coach away from Uffculme station forming the 2.45 pm Hemyock-Tiverton Junction service.

The station area has now been developed for housing, but little else appears to have changed in the village on 10 December 1993. *Peter W. Gray/David Mitchell*

HALBERTON HALT: Leaving Tiverton Junction on the other side of the main line was the branch to Tiverton, and the eastern end of the 109-foot-long platform at Halberton can be noted in this view from the road overbridge on 24 March 1962 as the 2.22 pm Tiverton Junction-Tiverton train arrives. The single auto-trailer is being propelled by 0-4-2T No 1471. Auto-train services commenced over this branch in 1927, while the '14XX' Class arrived in the autumn of 1932. The push-pull service was known locally as the 'Tivvy Bumper', and remained until the end of the branch passenger service.

Since closure the formation here has been totally assimilated into the adjoining fields, as can be seen on 26 December 1993. *Peter W. Gray/David Mitchell*

COWLEY BRIDGE JUNCTION: The signal box at the point where the GWR and LSWR lines parted company north of Exeter is prominent in this scene, taken on Whit Saturday, 20 May 1961, as 'Hall' 4-6-0 No 6940 *Didlington Hall* passes on a Wolverhampton to Kingswear service. The box dated from about 1894, when it replaced an earlier installation, and was extended at the north end in 1943 when the nearby Riverside Yard was also enlarged.

The closure and demolition of this well-known structure has at least provided train-watchers and photographers with a clearer view of the tracks. In this 21 May 1992 view, Class '37' No 37350 (the original D6700) is about to enter Riverside Yard with the 10.34 Fawley-Tavistock Junction train, conveying bitumen for Plymouth Cattewater and gas oil to BR depots in the South West. *Peter W. Gray/David Mitchell*

PULLABROOK HALT was opened on 1 June 1931 in an attempt by the Great Western to encourage additional traffic on the Moretonhampstead branch. Originally Hawkmoor, after a sanatorium which was actually some distance from the railway, it was renamed in June 1955. Less than four years later the final passenger services ran, and one of the last-day (28 February 1959) trains, the 12.50 pm Newton Abbot-Moretonhampstead, is pictured as it crosses a three-arch granite bridge just north of Pullabrook behind 0-4-2T No 1466.

Goods traffic to Moretonhampstead survived until April 1964, when the line closed completely north of Bovey. Unfortunately a preservation attempt failed, thus depriving future generations of the opportunity to travel over this scenic route. *Both Peter W. Gray*

CHURSTON station, on the Kingswear branch, was recorded at 10.23 am on 11 March 1960 just after the 10.15 am mixed train off the Brixham branch had arrived in the charge of '14XX' 0-4-2T No 1470. Other than fish trains that ran as required, by this time no exclusively freight service operated over the branch, and the goods traffic, mainly household coal, was included in the 7.35 am from Churston and this return working.

Since the first edition of 'British Railways Past and Present' No 8 was prepared, a new workshop has been erected by the Paignton & Dartmouth Steam Railway, and this rather dominates the present-day scene. This more modern image is completed on 20 June 1992 as the line's Class '25', No D7535, departs with a Kingswear to Paignton train during a Diesel Gala. *Peter W. Gray/David Mitchell*

CORNWALL LOOP JUNCTION: When the Cornwall Railway opened from Truro to Plymouth Millbay on 4 May 1859, it connected with the South Devon at Cornwall Junction, about half a mile north of the latter station. The LSWR opened a loop from Plymouth North Road to Cornwall Loop Junction in May 1876 for its trains to Devonport, enabling them to bypass Millbay. Subsequently the GWR also used this loop, and it became part of its main line to Cornwall. On 2 May 1959 an RCTS centenary railtour comprising No 6420 and auto-coaches is illustrated as it crosses Stonehouse Pool Viaduct on its way from Saltash to Millbay. Cornwall Loop Viaduct is on the right of the picture, while the original SDR route is out of sight below the photographer.

The curve from Cornwall Loop Junction to Cornwall Junction closed on 16 January 1964. The foreground has since been built up, and recently a dog-walking footpath and community green has been created. On 31 December 1993 the 10.35 Paddington-Penzance HST crosses Cornwall Loop Viaduct. Part of Stonehouse Pool Viaduct survives, and one of its girders (painted red) can be seen. *Peter W. Gray/David Mitchell*

Past and Present
Colour

Kent and East Sussex

BICKLEY: On a sunny 5 August 1957 two trains heading for the Kent coast pass Bickley station, both hauled by Maunsell-designed engines. Usually powered by a Bulleid 'Pacific', the 'Kentish Belle' Pullman from Victoria to Ramsgate is, on this occasion, entrusted to 'King Arthur' Class 4-6-0 No 30767 *Sir Valence*, the excursion being headed by work-stained Class 'N' 'Mogul' No 31404.

In an attempt to obtain two trains in similar positions, nearly two hours was spent at the same location on 8 January 1994, but luck did not prevail, and in the end it was necessary to make do with a single Class '423/1' 4VEP EMU, No 3446, which is proceeding away from the camera and running as the 13.00 service from Ashford to Victoria. The order of the 'up' and 'down' running lines here has been altered, and the signal box with its attendant semaphore signals has gone together with the telegraph poles; the position of the crossover lines has been moved, and the large tree on the right appears to have died. The change in nature's colours between summer and winter is also readily apparent. *R. C. Riley/Brian Morrison*

ST MARY CRAY: Soon after the two-track section of the line at this location had been doubled, BR Standard Class '5MT' 4-6-0 No 73083 *Pendragon* passes through the newly created cutting near St Mary Cray on 18 May 1959, hauling a train from Ramsgate to Victoria.

In the summer months it is now impossible to duplicate the position from which this photograph was taken, but on 13 March 1994 the tree branches are still devoid of leaves, and allow a view of Class '423/1' 4VEP No 3451 passing the same spot and forming a Sunday train from Margate to Victoria, rescheduled as a result of weekend engineering works. Apart from the absence of semaphore signalling, the concrete cutting walls have discoloured over the years, and the banking is almost unrecognisable. *R. C. Riley/Brian Morrison*

ST MARY CRAY JUNCTION: With the third rail electric current obviously switched off, track maintenance men (then still known as gangers) await the passing of a summer additional working from Victoria to Hastings on 16 May 1959, hauled by 'Schools' Class 4-4-0 No 30937 *Epsom*.

Seen from the same footbridge on 15 January 1994 Class '319/0' 'Thameslink' EMU No 319024 forms the 08.33 train from Bedford to Sevenoaks. The colour change from summer to winter is again self-evident, as is the complete obliteration of the banking on the left by trees and bushes. *R. C. Riley/Brian Morrison*

TONBRIDGE SHED: On the day before the official end of main-line steam operation to the Kent coast, on 12 June 1961, the engine shed of Tonbridge (then designated 73J) contained (from left to right) a Bulleid 'Q1' Class 0-6-0, ex-works Class 'L1' 4-4-0 No 31786, Class 'N1' 'Mogul' No 31877, Class 'N' 'Mogul' No 31871, 0-6-0 diesel shunter No D3044 (later Class '08' No 08032), another Wainwright 'Mogul', and another 0-6-0 diesel shunter, Class '12' No 15220.

Currently nothing remains of the shed, the site being occupied as a storage place for BR Civil Engineer's tools and accoutrements. The Hastings line on the right is all that remains as a point of reference between the two scenes, the present one being photographed on 26 January 1994. *R. C. Riley/Brian Morrison*

ASHFORD: With BR Standard Class '4MT' 2-6-4T No 80065 shunting in the background, the 07.24 train from London Bridge to Ramsgate makes the scheduled stop at Ashford station on 14 May 1960 headed by Class 'D1' 4-4-0 No 31489.

With station improvements under way on 13 March 1994, an equivalent service from Charing Cross to Ramsgate was formed by Class '411/5' 4CEP No 1572. *R. C. Riley/Brian Beer*

RAMSGATE: Shunting empty coaching stock at Ramsgate, Class 'C' 0-6-0 No 31245 runs alongside Ramsgate shed (then designated 73G) on 28 March 1959.

The shed was closed to steam later the same year and converted to maintain EMU stock. The original building outline has been maintained for the EMU depot, but there has been extensive remodelling, with the walls now brick-clad and new-style windows incorporated. On 6 March 1994 a Class '421' 4CIG is stabled outside the depot on the same track, as Class '411/5' 4CEP No 1524 travels under the same bridge, departing from the station at the rear of the 15.45 service to Charing Cross. The switched-on headlight is a staff oversight! *R. C. Riley/Brian Morrison*

SHEPHERDS WELL: Hauling a four-coach train from Faversham to Dover, Wainwright Class 'L' 4-4-0 No 31768 slows for the Shepherds Well stop on 23 March 1959.

In the same position on 6 March 1994 Class '411/5' 4CEP No 1552 forms the 12.41 train from Victoria to Dover Western Docks. Although the signal box is still operational, the goods shed, semaphore signal and siding on the right have all become victims of the passing years. A lorry replaces the Morris Minor car in the car park, the 'Southern' station sign has been replaced with a NSE type, and the trees have grown upwards to some extent. The two boys are not thought to be related! *R. C. Riley/Brian Beer*

NEWHAVEN TOWN: Approaching Newhaven Town station and passing the signal box of the same name, a Railway Correspondence & Travel Society special train of 7 October 1962 is hauled over the gated level crossing by 'A1X' Class 'Terrier' 0-6-0T No 32636 piloting Class 'E6' 0-6-2T No 32418.

Now in NSE guise, the signal box still exists to operate what is now a barrier crossing controlling the widened road, although a new road bridge scars the scene to take the majority of traffic over the line to avoid the crossing. With the old telegraph poles and attendant wiring no longer in evidence, the 10.43 train from Brighton to Seaford slows for the station stop on 13 March 1994, formed of Class '421/4' 4CIG No 1855. *R. C. Riley/Brian Morrison*

KINGHAM was the junction of the 'Cotswold Line' from Oxford to Evesham and Worcester and the Banbury & Cheltenham Direct line which crossed the former at right angles, two south-facing chords linking the two. With the B&CDR bridge in the background, 'Hall' Class 4-6-0 No 5957 *Hutton Hall* and 'Castle' Class 4-6-0 No 5099 *Clifford Castle* arrive with a Hereford to Paddington service on 19 May 1962. On the right are the bay platforms for the Cheltenham and Chipping Norton services, the through service east to Banbury having been withdrawn in 1951. Services on the B&CDR ceased completely later in 1962.

Today only basic facilities are provided at Kingham and the station is staffed only on a part-time basis. *Both Laurence Waters*

OXFORD GENERAL (GWR): '7400' Class 2-6-2T No 4103 stands at the south end of the station on 12 June 1960 with the 1.20 pm service from Oxford to Princes Risborough.

The old station was removed in 1971 and replaced by a temporary structure, which lasted until 1990 when a more permanent station was constructed. In August 1991 a pair of Class '47s', Nos 47636 and 47827, depart from the new station with a Network Express service to London. *Both Tony Doyle*

THAME was the most important intermediate station on the line to Princes Risborough, and boasted a Brunel-designed overall roof. This can be seen on a snowy 5 January 1963 as '6100' Class 2-6-2T No 6111 waits with the same train as in the previous photograph, the 1.20 pm Oxford-Princes Risborough.

The station closed to passengers on the following day and was soon removed. The line has survived, and today is single track and the only trace of the old station is the platform edging. *Both Laurence Waters*

EYNSHAM stood on the branch to Fairford, heading west from Oxford via Yarnton Junction. On 16 March 1961 '5700' Class 0-6-0PT No 4649 stands in the station with the 8.55 am service to Oxford.

Eynsham was closed to passengers on 18 June 1962 and to goods on 26 April 1965. Today the trackbed forms a service road into the large Oxford Instruments factory. *Both Tony Doyle*

WITNEY was a few miles further east and was the principal station on the branch. In this delightful scene we see the 8.23 am service from Carterton to Oxford arriving behind '7400' Class 0-6-0PT No 7412 on 19 May 1962.

Since the line closed on 18 June 1962 the station site has been levelled and is now an industrial estate. Nothing remains to link the two views. *Laurence Waters/Tony Doyle*

HINKSEY NORTH: South of Oxford on the main line were extensive sidings. On 28 July 1964 'Castle' Class 4-6-0 No 5056 *Earl of Powis* passes Hinksey Yard with an up parcels train to Paddington via Princes Risborough.

Once overshadowed by the Oxford Gasworks, the skyline has changed somewhat in July 1992 as Thames Turbo No 165112 departs with the 1.00 pm service to Paddington. *Both Tony Doyle*

RADLEY, between Oxford and Didcot, was junction for the short Abingdon branch, trains for which used the bay platform where this LCGB branch line special stands behind 0-6-0PT No 9773 on 15 August 1965. The sidings on the left were used for stabling the branch stock.

Passenger services on the branch were withdrawn in 1963, although goods traffic lingered on until 1984. Today Radley is an unstaffed halt, and the bay lines, removed in 1974, are used as a car park. *Both Tony Doyle*

DIDCOT: A fine view of '6100' Class 2-6-2T No 6139 on station pilot duty on 18 October 1962. The same spot has in recent years been used as a stabling point for Railfreight locomotives, and on 8 August 1991 a pair of Class '37' diesels, Nos 37230 and 37258, await their next turn of duty. *Both Tony Doyle*

Past and Present Colour

East Anglia

CROMER BEACH: One day in the late 1960s the driver and guard of a Norwich to Sheringham train pause for a chat in the sunshine at Cromer Beach. Trains on this service have to reverse here, the former M&GN terminus. The driver is changing cabs, while the guard is transferring the tail lamp from one end of the train to the other. *Graham H. Smith*

Nowadays the former goods yard and loco shed area are occupied by a supermarket development, giving a far more cramped appearance to the station. The platform has been shortened, and the overall roof demolished, while the station building is threatened with demolition. In November 1993 a Class '156' squeezes in between the supermarket wall and the platforms - but despite all the alterations, the driver still has to change cabs here, and is seen with the single line token. *Des Saunders*

FAKENHAM EAST: In the 1970s a daily goods train hauled by a Class '31' trundled along the old Wells-next-the-Sea branch as far as Fakenham GE station, where the track terminated in the cutting north of the station. This train very often consisted of a couple of trucks and a brake-van, and the crew used to lunch in the old station buildings, at that time a temporary office used by the Eastern Counties bus company.

Today the site is unrecognisable, but the photographer is standing on approximately the same spot where he stood nearly 20 years ago; it is now a sheltered housing complex with a resident warden. *Both Des Saunders*

NORWICH THORPE: Apart from the removal of the coaling facility, the approaches to Norwich Thorpe station remained surprising unchanged through the post-war years, until the area was remodelled in connection with the 1987 electrification. This was the busy scene on 23 April 1985, with a Class '101' DMU leaving on a local service, as a Class '47' stands in the headshunt between duties on the London service, and No 45044 waits for the road with a lengthy mixed goods train for Whitemoor.

Almost exactly three years later, No 37708 and No 37889 double-head an oil train out of the goods yard over considerably simplified trackwork on to the electrified main line. With the signal boxes gone, the whole area is now controlled from Colchester power box, some 80 miles away. *Both Richard Adderson*

LOWESTOFT: A busy scene on 2 May 1970, with passengers on platform 4 alighting from one of the rare Wickham-built DMUs, and mingling with others waiting to board their train for the return journey to Norwich. The Cravens unit in platform 2 is operating the shuttle service to and from Yarmouth South Town, a service which was to run for the last time later that day.

What a difference the removal of the overall station roof makes! Despite much local opposition, the historic wooden structure was removed in 1992, leaving the waiting passengers at the mercy of the elements; with the North Sea only a few hundred yards away, Lowestoft station can be a very cold place indeed. Nevertheless, the town is still served by trains on two different routes: inland to Norwich, and southward along the East Suffolk line to Ipswich. A sunny November day in 1993 sees a Class '156' on the East Suffolk line service. *Both Richard Adderson*

ELY: On a November morning in 1969 Brush Type 2 No D5854, newly repainted in blue livery, waits amongst the semaphore signals at Ely with a Liverpool Street to Kings Lynn express. *Richard Adderson*

Ely station was remodelled with the electrification of the Kings Lynn line in 1992, and platform 1 was extended outwards, over the former platform line, in order to give clearance for the overhead electrification without cutting back the platform canopies. In November 1993 a Class '158' unit on an Ipswich to Leicester working is seen leaving the platform. It is good to see that this East Anglian railway crossroads is still busy - the rather eerie warning notes of the level crossing are not silent for long, and the photographer saw five trains pass while the barriers remained closed. *Des Saunders*

ST IVES: There is quite a crowd on the platform as the driver of a last-day train exchanges the single-line token as he runs into St Ives in October 1970. The platform to the left once served trains to Huntingdon. *Richard Adderson*

There is now an absolute wilderness where this pleasant junction station once stood. A southern bypass separates the station area from a part of the old station still standing and used as offices; the photographer had to make a quick dash across the road to get the picture. An old railway house - probably the Station Master's house - remains in private occupation to the right. *Des Saunders*

FELIXSTOWE TOWN: A Cravens DMU on the Ipswich shuttle service stands at the buffers at Felixstowe Town on 14 March 1970, while the brake-van beyond is evidence that goods trains still used the station to reverse on their way to the docks. *Richard Adderson*

The old station has been completely refurbished and is now a tasteful shopping centre and mini-market, but its former life cannot be disguised: the ticket barrier where yesteryear's DMU stood is clearly visible, but the track has been taken back to a simple shelter some 200 yards to the west, and now stands in a car park. *Des Saunders*

MISTLEY: In the early 1980s Mistley station, on the Harwich branch, was described as the best remaining example of a Great Eastern country station. The station itself was well kept and staffed on certain shifts, while the scene from the up end of the platform oozed atmosphere, with the semaphore signals, working signal box, and the active goods yard. No 31178 approaches with a train from Peterborough to Parkeston Quay in 1984.

The Harwich branch was electrified in 1986, changing the scene entirely. Semaphores, signal box and most of the sidings have disappeared, but the chimney of the Edme malt extract works continues to look down on the scene, as a Class '321' EMU passes in November 1993. *Both Richard Adderson*

Past and Present Colour

South and West Yorkshire

ST DUNSTAN'S, BRADFORD, closed in September 1952, but the remains of the station platforms can still be seen in this June 1967 picture showing a Class '24' diesel piloting a Fairburn 2-6-4T on a Bradford Exchange-King's Cross train during the transition from steam to diesel power. The train is climbing steeply on the sharp curve of the former GNR line to Leeds, having just diverged from the former LYR route to Halifax and Manchester, which can be seen behind the rear coaches. Directly behind St Dunstan's signal box on the left are lines leading to the carriage sidings, and also the GNR route to Halifax and Keighley via Queensbury, from which passenger services were withdrawn in May 1955. Some wagons in Springmill Street coal yard, approached from the LYR line, are visible in the left distance.

In the April 1992 picture Class '47' No 47489 is heading a short van train from what is now Bradford Interchange station to Leeds, having just passed a Class '158' unit on a service from Leeds. The signal box and all the semaphore signalling has now gone, and the GNR Queensbury route and carriage sidings in the vicinity of St Dunstan's have been removed and the site landscaped. Mill Lane signal box, however, still exists, and controls Interchange station and the junction of the Manchester and Leeds lines. *Both John S. Whiteley*

SHIPLEY, BRADFORD JUNCTION: In June 1967 'Britannia' 'Pacific' No 70004 (formerly William Shakespeare) approaches adverse signals with the evening freight from Valley Road, Bradford, to Carlisle. The triangular junction at Shipley is formed by the lines from Bradford Forster Square to Leeds and to Skipton, linked by the direct line between those two places via the Aire Valley, which was built by the Midland Railway and bypassed Bradford. The semaphore signals of the junction can be seen, together with the extensive trackwork and goods shed on the left; Shipley, Leeds Junction signal box is just visible in the distance above the first wagon.

By 22 June 1990 the trackwork has been rationalised as Class '47' No 47407 hauls the 15.50 King's Cross-Bradford Forster Square away from its stop at Shipley. DVT No 82205 is behind the '47', and Class '91' electric No 91004 is at the rear, the train having been electrically hauled as far as Leeds, where it reversed for the remainder of the journey to Bradford. The yard on the left is occupied by a scrap-metal merchant, and at the time of writing work is progressing on the overhead electrification of the line from Leeds to Ilkley, Bradford Forster Square and Skipton, which will again transform this scene. *Both John S. Whiteley*

SHIPLEY, BINGLEY JUNCTION: Class '9F' 2-10-0 No 92234 passes in March 1967 with coal empties from Carlisle to Leeds. The line in the foreground is the west chord of the triangle and leads to Bradford Forster Square; the platforms are just out of the right-hand side of the picture beyond the signal box. The semaphore signals are set for Shipley, Leeds Junction, the roof of which signal box is partly visible above the exhaust of the '9F'. The east side of the triangle can be seen in the right background.

For some reason the Midland Railway did not construct platforms on the north side of the triangle, the direct Skipton-Leeds line, but in 1979 one platform was provided on the down side, which not surprisingly resulted in some operating difficulties involving a section of 'wrong line' working for Leeds-bound trains. However, sense ultimately prevailed, and in 1992 a platform was provided on the up line together with a footbridge linking the two and an extensive car park in the centre of the triangle. This has resulted in considerable extra business from this now busy station, although only one platform survives on the Skipton line, track on that side of the triangle having been singled. In the modern photograph a unit approaches one of the new platforms with a Skipton-Leeds service, and the station and signal box are now in West Yorkshire PTE colours. *Both John S. Whiteley*

WORTLEY JUNCTION, LEEDS: It is not possible to repeat the picture of '4F' 0-6-0 No 44238 today as it was taken from the signal box steps on 5 June 1963, and the box vanished in around 1968. However, today one can still get a good view from the footbridge that crosses the railway and dual carriageway, but this is likely to change in the very near future when the wires go up for the Aire Valley electrification scheme. The sidings on the right used to serve a gas works, while those on the left were for the coal yard; the lines that curved off to the left joined the main line into Leeds Central.

Thirty years on there are only four tracks serving the Harrogate line and that to the north via Shipley. On 15 November 1993 a West Yorkshire PTE Class '141' unit is seen heading north; the signal box used to be situated at the end of the brick wall. *Both Gavin Morrison*

STOURTON, LEEDS: On 21 August 1979, in the days when the signal box and wagon repair depot were still in operation, a Class '101' Metro-Cammell DMU, in the short-lived white and blue striped livery, heads for Leeds. The old steam depot, code 55B, was situated to the right of the picture.

Today there is virtually nothing left other than the freightliner terminal, which is still very active. On a misty 15 November 1993 a West Yorkshire PTE Class '141' unit heads south. *Both Gavin Morrison*

HEATON LODGE JUNCTION, MIRFIELD, boasted a splendid array of semaphore signals, some of which can be seen in this picture of '8F' 2-8-0 No 48448 taking coal empties from Wyre Dock to Healey Mills on 6 April 1968. The LNWR trans-Pennine route between Manchester and Leeds met the LYR Calder Valley route to Manchester at this point, and the two companies ran side by side on this busy section of line to Ravensthorpe, almost two miles to the east of Mirfield station. Because of the congestion on this short section of railway, and the desire to seek new traffic in the Spen Valley, the LNWR built a new route from Heaton Lodge Junction to Leeds via Gomersal. Opened to passengers in 1900, it was known as the 'Leeds New Line'. Although passenger traffic was withdrawn in 1953, it remained open until 31 July 1965 as a relief route, and can be seen here behind the '8F' at a slightly higher level. During the early 1970s the junction was remodelled, but a short section of the 'New Line' and its underpass were retained to segregate Manchester-Leeds via Huddersfield passenger traffic from Calder Valley route freight.

The high embankment at Heaton Lodge was a favourite vantage point to observe passing trains, but today the old familiar view has largely been obliterated by trees, and the down goods line has been lifted. On 15 November 1993 a Class '142' 'Pacer' heads for Wakefield along the 'New Line', the track of which has been moved to provide a junction with the old route, and is now single and used by down services. *John S. Whiteley/Gavin Morrison*

NORMANTON was a very busy centre until the mid-1960s, when the former Midland line went through to Sheffield and traffic was heavy between York and the Calder Valley. By 25 July 1983, when Class '40' No 40004 passed through with a special to East Anglia, the original buildings were in a terrible state, and the extensive marshalling yards had been lifted.

The buildings were eventually demolished and the familiar red West Yorkshire PTE 'bus shelter' erected on the old platform base. On 15 November 1993 Class '141' No 141120 leaves for Sheffield. *Both Gavin Morrison*

WINCOBANK & MEADOWHALL, SHEFFIELD: On 14 September 1975 No 4472 *Flying Scotsman* **has just passed Wincobank Station Junction with a special from Sheffield to Newcastle. It is taking the route via Rotherham, and the line to Barnsley can be seen diverging to the right beyond the rear of the train.**

The steelworks of this industrial city have been decimated during the last 20 years or so, and many no longer exist, as can be seen in this November 1993 picture. The scene is now dominated by the enormous Meadowhall shopping complex with its acres of adjacent car parking. In the distance a unit can be seen at Meadowhall station, and in the foreground a Class '156' unit has just left the station with a service from Sheffield to Hull via Rotherham and Doncaster. The line with overhead electrification alongside the railway is the first section of the Sheffield Supertram system, which is due to commence operating from the city centre to the Meadowhall complex in late 1993. *Both John S. Whiteley*

Past and Present Colour

Cleveland and North Yorkshire

GOATHLAND, NYMR: The early experimentation with traction sources of our first post-nationalisation private railways can perhaps, with hindsight, seem rather naive, but nevertheless showed the fighting determination that prevailed at the time to start running with whatever was available. Prominent here on the fledgling North Yorkshire Moors Railway in 1970 is a four-wheel German-built forerunner of today's BR 'Pacer' trains, although in single-car form. These units saw brief spells in diverse areas of BR, in particular East Anglia, in an attempt to save certain branch lines from the Beeching 'pogroms' that devastated rural areas. Behind, 'Phillie tank' No 29 (once of the NCB installation at Philadelphia, Co Durham) stands awaiting trials, and now in its first black coat. Further back can be seen Class 'Q6' No 63395.

It is not possible to repeat the scene exactly because of bush and tree growth in the intervening years, but this recent view illustrates just how the infrastructure has been left generally faithful to the early inherited conditions. North Eastern Locomotive Preservation Group-owned Class 'K1' No 2005 arrives with the 15.20 hrs Pickering-Grosmont service, and meets 'Warship' diesel-hydraulic No D821 *Greyhound* about to depart with the 15.55 hrs return service. The temporary engine standage area has now given way to coaching stock of all types and hue. Signals remain the same, but the pole route has gone. *E. E. Smith, courtesy Veronica Pybus/Peter J. Robinson*

EAGLESCLIFFE: Here we see a comparison in container modes. In September 1965 a Class 'Q6' plods along the once heavily used four-track stretch between Eaglescliffe and Bowesfield Junction with dolomite containers from Thrislington Quarry (Ferryhill) bound for the Steetley Steel Works at Hartlepool Cemetery North. The square inter-modal containers, loaded three to a flat, were a result of 1950s joint co-operation between Middlesbrough's Divisional Manager and Steetley's.

The line once occupied by a steady procession of 'Q6' and 'WD' steam locos is now a siding, while a Wilton-Leeds Freightliner, hauled by Railfreight Distribution engines Nos 37073 and 37101, provides colour to an otherwise grey railway scene as it passes on 15 June 1992. It could be argued that this freight form is the direct descendent of the now distant dolomite containers. *John M. Boyes, John Gilks collection/Peter J. Robinson*

CARGO FLEET, MIDDLESBROUGH: With Cochrane's iron and steel works publicising its name upon its water tower, one of the company's diminutive 0-4-0ST locos (*Cochrane's No 6*) stands alone on the exchange sidings while the crew walk back to the shed, having left 'L'-plates adorning the little engine. What seems to be an ex-railway Scammel in maroon livery stands close by, while the black mass of Cargo Fleet BSC Works looms above a host of mineral wagons in the far distance. The date is 24 August 1967.

By 29 December 1993 Whitehouse Crossing cabin and a now weathered perimeter fence provide the main continuity features across the 26 years of industrial decline in the surrounding landscape. Where once stood the little tank engine now lies the path of the advancing far-side fencing. In RFD livery, Class '47' No 47378 goes west towards Wilton to take up Freightliner 4D50 for Leeds FLT. *John M. Boyes, John Gilks collection/Peter J. Robinson*

STOCKTON ON TEES: Controlling traffic on the six through routes on 11 April 1965 is Bishopton Lane cabin. Opposite is a row of railway-inspired houses that literally gave employees a 'walk-on part', for they stood in the cess, at one time without even a guard-rail in sight.

Stockton hung on to through express services until the 1980s, when HSTs continued to use the route but didn't call. Back in the '60s we see one of the frequent Newcastle-Liverpool semi-fasts in the charge of a Gateshead 'Peak' Class diesel calling at the station. In the distant yards 16-ton mineral wagons await their call-up to Thompson's scrapyard round the far bend. These are the last moments of Stockton's rail heyday, and although not the site where railways 'began', this station was nevertheless the face that represented the start of it all to thousands of members of the travelling public.

The sad contrast from today's viewpoint says it all. The chagrin felt locally for what represented Stockton's claim to fame increased with the crumbling of the station and subsequent orgy of vandalism visited upon the remains. Only recently have Stockton Town Council and British Rail begun to plan a phoenix-like resuscitation plan. Newcastle-Middlesbrough units continue to link Stockton with the provinces, but a more optimistic freight outlook is represented on 29 December 1993 by a Class '60' on the last leg of its journey with train 6N39 from Leeds to Port Clarence Phillips oil terminal. *John M. Boyes, John Gilks collection/Peter J. Robinson*

RAVENSCAR, at the summit of the Scarborough & Whitby Railway, opened to the public in 1885. In the view above we see the station in its last years, on a cold and blustery 1 October 1963. An enthusiasts' special gives an opportunity to say farewell and provide a final chance to survey what for many was the holiday line of their childhood. The enginemen of the York-based Class 'B1' engines make use of the photographic pause to make steam; the locos are Nos 61031 *Reedbuck* and 61018 *Gnu*.

Thirty years on from that steam special, in December 1993 (*below*), a black and white cat surveys post-railway foliage from a perch on the old perimeter wall while the houses and the gate (turned 180 degrees from its former position) link the past with the present.

Ravenscar station closed from 8 March 1965. Four days before (*opposite*), the 07.20 hrs Middlesbrough-Scarborough DMU arrives at an empty platform (one side was stone, the other wooden planking), this time in fine coastal weather. *John Gilks collection/Dave Tyreman/Peter J. Robinson*

GROSMONT SHED, NYMR: Finally, we return to the preserved North Yorkshire Moors Railway year. In 1969, having secured the infrastructure, one of the first requirements of the NYMR Management Committee was to give shelter and maintenance facilities to the motive power of the NELPG and other individuals who were to get the first trains moving. Prominent in this view is No 5, the first of the two 'Phillie tanks' to be 'dressed' for public service, while sister engine No 29 stands behind awaiting completion by resident painter and photographer Kevin Hudspith.

While we have broken a ground-rule of the series by not repeating the current view from exactly the same position, it has given us the opportunity to show not only No 5 in the self-same spot, but also something hardly envisaged in the 1960s - 'Deltics' on a full day's work on an 18-mile branch that was not even directly joined to the ECML. In this case it is No 55015 masquerading as 55018 *Ballymoss* during the NYMR Diesel Gala Day of 18 September 1993. *E. E. Smith, courtesy Veronica Pybus/Peter J. Robinson*

South East Scotland

*All 'past' photographs by
K. M. Falconer;
all 'present' photographs by
Keith Sanders.*

EDINBURGH WAVERLEY: A classic picture of an 'A4'.'Pacific' standing at the east end of Waverley station. The occasion was the working of 'A3' No 4472 *Flying Scotsman* with a Pullman train organised by the locomotive's then owner, Alan Pegler. *Flying Scotsman* was to remain in Scotland for a couple of weeks, so No 60009 *Union of South Africa* was to work the special back to the south. The date is 9 May 1964, and the train is standing in platform 8.

Platforms 8 and 9 are now used exclusively for Motorail vans, and the only bay platform at the east end that is used for public services is platform 7, into which EMU No 305501 is running with the 13.20 hrs from North Berwick on 7 January 1994. The skyline is unaltered, but the old North British Hotel has been stone-cleaned and is now known as the Balmoral.

NIDDRIE NORTH: On 28 August 1964 Standard 2-6-4T No 80054 is working the 6.11 pm from Esk Bank to Edinburgh Waverley. The outward working was the 5.11 pm Waverley to Gorebridge; at the latter the loco ran round the train and worked the empty stock to Esk Bank to form the 6.11 pm. The train is seen passing under the 'Lothian Lines', opened in 1915 and closed in 1967. The 'Lothian Lines' allowed freight trains to leave the East Coast Main Line then take either a spur to Niddrie West Junction, or to swing round to the right and cross the lines in the picture, then cross over the ECML in order to drop down into the back of the Portobello yards.

Today the scene is much changed. The single line to the right remains and is part of the suburban circle (the 'Sub'), while the lines on the left have been singled and wired. Niddrie North signal box survived until 6 May 1973, and operated both the upper and lower lines. The only remnants of the 'Lothian Lines' are the brick bridge piers. All trace of Newcraighall Colliery, in the background, has been erased.

PORTOBELLO EAST JUNCTION: A Birmingham RCW Type 2 diesel is seen leaving the East Coast Main Line and swinging on to the Waverley Route with the 4.10 pm Edinburgh Waverley-Hawick service on 17 August 1968. The bridge over the ECML in the background carried the 'Lothian Lines'.

The junction layout is now much simplified, much of the remodelling having been carried out in 1971. A Class '91' is seen propelling the 10.00 hrs Edinburgh Waverley-London King's Cross on 4 January 1994. The trackbed of the 'Lothian Lines' is now a road - Sir Harry Lauder Way.

CRAIGENTINNY: 'V2' No 60891 runs past the west end of the large carriage depot with the York-Edinburgh parcels on 20 August 1961. In the depot two Birmingham RCW Type 2 diesels wait with empty stock, which will probably form an Edinburgh-Aberdeen train. The main line consisted of four tracks at this point, the furthest pair being freight lines to and from Portobello yards.

The present-day photograph has been taken from a higher vantage point, and shows the revised track layout. The main line is now two tracks only, and occupies the trackbed of the old freight lines. EMU No 305501 is passing with the 10.20 hrs from North Berwick on 4 January 1994. In the sidings are Nos 37214 and 37080 awaiting their next duties. All lines in the depot are now 'under the wires'.

MILLERHILL: Astride the Waverley Route, to the east of Edinburgh, were these large hump marshalling yards, opened in 1962; the up reception yards are visible on the right as D5313 heads south on the main line on 24 July 1963 with a freight consisting mainly of short-wheelbase vans.

Today the yards are much reduced and are used as storing and holding sidings while crew and loco changes take place. As can be seen, the access from the north is just two running lines, and while these have been wired it is not known if any electrically hauled freights have entered the yard. The main change is the bypass road in the background, which is now part of the A1.

BORTHWICK: On 8 April 1968, just nine months before the Waverley Route closed, a Birmingham RCW Type 2 diesel drops down Borthwick Bank with the 1.00 pm Carlisle-Edinburgh. Going south from Hardengreen Junction the ruling gradient was 1 in 70 for just over 9 miles to the summit at Falahill. Borthwick was about 3 miles from the summit.

On a wintry 8 January 1994 the scene is little changed apart from the loss of the railway. However, careful inspection revealed that the platelayers' hut still survived behind the bush.

FALKLAND ROAD station was a mile from the summit of the climb from Ladybank to Lochmuir box, on the Tay Bridge to Edinburgh line. On Good Friday, 16 April 1965, 'A3' No 60100 *Spearmint* heads up the grade with return empty stock from a King's Cross-Aberdeen relief. The station closed to passengers on 15 September 1958, and to freight on 14 February 1965, when the signal box was also lost. *Spearmint* was withdrawn on 19 June 1965, just over two months after this picture was taken.

The station building has survived intact, and on 4 January 1994 the modern railway is represented by 'Express Sprinter' unit No 158739 with the 13.10 hrs Edinburgh-Aberdeen service.

KELTY: Looking north towards Kelty Colliery (pictured on page 78 of 'Past and Present' No 9), a BR Sulzer Type 2 heads the 8.15 am Inverness-Edinburgh service on 16 April 1965. A 'J38' 0-6-0 is standing in the up loop. The direct line from the Forth Bridge to Perth closed to passengers on 4 January 1970, and completely a few months later.

Exactly 24 years to the day after closure, 4 January 1994, we see that the railway has been completely removed and the area landscaped. The electricity sub-station in the field used to be within the colliery.

Having eventually concluded my professional studies - which had been constantly interrupted because of my love of railways - I spent a short spell working at the District Valuer's Office in Bradford. This office was also very conveniently situation, only a short distance from the line into Forster Square station, which was consequently given considerably more attention than the properties which I was supposed to be acquiring for Local Authority redevelopment. The afternoon 'Carlisle slow' produced a variety of different motive power and during this period in the early 1960s there was a considerable amount of parcels traffic handled at Forster Square station. Sadly, all this has now disappeared, leaving only two platforms operational, for use on local DMU services.

While I derived a great deal of enjoyment from helping to prepare the 'Past and Present' book, it was nevertheless a rather sad task in some ways. Certainly modern stock and locomotives, including BR's impressive HST units, grace some of the local main lines, and while the 'new generation' DMU trains maintain secondary services, it is also true that much of what I came to love about the railways of South and West Yorkshire (and indeed across the country generally) has been slowly destroyed. Regrettably the process still continues, although in recent times there has been a welcome awakening of public opposition to what is happening, notably concerning the Settle-Carlisle line, and it is to be hoped that this opposition will have a constructive effect. Otherwise, who knows what else will have disappeared in another 20 years?

Gavin Morrison then takes up the story.

Most of my life has been spent in the area covered by this book, in particular the West Riding of Yorkshire, and helping to compile it was therefore very enjoyable. Nevertheless, it forcibly brought home to me how many railway features that I (and I'm sure many others) had once taken for granted have now gone for ever. Like so many things in life, it is only when something has gone that you fully appreciate how much it was a part of your life. Notwithstanding that, I still derive much pleasure from photographing current British Rail operations and no doubt many of the photographs that we took in the 1980s will be of historical importance sooner than we might expect.

My most vivid early memories of steam locomotives at work in Britain are at Glasgow Central during the Second World War, when I watched the dirty LMS 'Pacifics' arriving and leaving with their trains. One other occasion in particular stands out in my mind, and that was when in 1943 I was travelling from Leeds to Glasgow St Enoch, and the first rebuilt 'Royal Scot', 4-6-0 No 6103 *Royal Scots Fusilier*, backed on to our train at Leeds City station. The locomotive caused me much confusion as no photograph could be found in my Ian Allan 'ABC' to identify it, and it was some time before I sorted out the mystery!

I lived for many years at Ovenden, about three miles out of Halifax, on the old Great Northern/Lancashire & Yorkshire Joint Line, and I was therefore brought up on a railway 'diet' of GNR 'N1' 0-6-2Ts and 'C12' 4-4-2Ts, together with Fowler 0-8-0s, and LYR 0-6-0s. The memories I have of these locomotives thrashing their way up the 1 in 50 gradients will always remain with me and, indeed, it was on the Holmfield-Pellon line that I first experienced the thrill of my first footplate ride, aboard Fowler 0-8-0 No 49540, of Sowerby Bridge depot.

I did have a few years away from Yorkshire when I lived for a time in North Wales and Worcester. In Wales I was lucky enough to see the last of the LNWR passenger locomotives at work, and I vividly recall the immaculate Worcester 'Castle' 4-6-0s, and the Hereford 'Hall' 4-6-0s, not to mention a few 'Saints' and 'Stars'.

My first job in Bradford offered little opportunity for railway activity, but this changed when I moved to Brighouse, near the Calder Valley main line. Fortunately the lunch break coincided with the passing of the premier train of the day, the 10.30 am Liverpool Exchange-Newcastle, so I became well acquainted with the famous Bank Hall trio of 'Jubilees', Nos 45698 *Mars*, 45717 *Dauntless* and 46719 *Glorious*, together with the same shed's unrebuilt 'Patriot' 4-6-0 No 45517.

In 1960 I joined what was then the National Cash Register Company, in Leeds, as a salesman, and this gave me considerable flexibility during the day, and I travelled extensively in the Yorkshire area. I took full advantage of this opportunity and managed to photograph most of the main-line steam traction operating out of Leeds at this time, before the diesels arrived in late 1960 and 1961. The first examples of diesel traction we saw in the area were Class '45' and '40' types.

I was fortunate to make many friends on the railway at this time, and there was little of interest that occurred in daylight hours that I did not get to hear about, or as happened on several occasions, was arranged for my benefit. Probably the most unusual of all events was the time I received a phone call from 'Control' during tea one Saturday afternoon, informing me that a GWR 'Grange' had just passed Penistone and was *en route* to Huddersfield. Knowing it was definitely not 1 April, tea was immediately terminated and I was at Huddersfield station within 15 minutes to see the train arrive and witness the damage to the cylinder casings where the locomotive had struck the platform edges along the way!

After steam finished on BR metals my railway photography virtually ceased, apart from trips abroad and endless visits to the Keighley & Worth Valley Railway. I now deeply regret this period of inactivity, but in 1975 I purchase my Pentax '6x7' camera, which completely revived my interest, and I was soon back at the lineside recording the modern scene. Now my photography is back to the same level of intensity that it was during the steam years of the 1960s.

Times are very different for the railway photographer today compared with 30 or so years ago, when it was a very lonely hobby.

Then I could spend a whole day at the lineside on the Settle-Carlisle line, or on Shap Fell, and never see another soul. How different it is today! I do miss the past, in particular the railwaymen - the drivers and firemen at Holbeck depot whom I got to know so well - and I was privileged to witness first-hand their skills in handling steam over the 'S&C'. Their everyday craft is sadly missed today. It isn't quite the same with HSTs or Class '47s', but one must look forward to the future, and not dwell too much in the past. The railways of South and West Yorkshire still have much to offer the railway enthusiast and photographer, and hopefully they will continue to do so for many years to come.

CLEVELAND AND NORTH YORKSHIRE

Alan R. Thompson & Ken Groundwater

This is an area of deep industrial tradition wherein families still boast of a lineage back to Stockton & Darlington roots or connections with the great 'ironmasters' of the

19th century. It cannot be disputed that, in industrial terms, the area certainly made an impression nationally, and the railway, as the 'father', the catalyst, was eventually eclipsed by the 'child' or, to put it bluntly, one hundred furnaces that lit the Yorkshire night skies like the Northern Lights. Railway stories from the area abound, but one in particular tells us that during an (early) inter-Union dispute the loyalty of railwaymen here was hard pressed and resulted in someone (from the LNWR?) coining them 'pease-pudding men', clearly reflecting the influence of one remarkable Quaker family upon the workforce and the area.

This is perhaps something of an understatement as it was Edward Pease who facilitated the eventual growth of Tees-side when, viewing a cluster of buildings at a place called Middlesbrough Farm, he said 'Some day we will export coal from here - someday. . .', eventually steering the 'Middlesbrough Owners' into securing more than 500 acres that became the nucleus of the town.

What came over strongly during our area study were the incredible contradictions within a relatively small corner of England; contradictions not only in landscape but in the way that man's labours are intensified all the more by the fact that chemist and steelmaster share the neighbourhood with farmer and fisherman. At one extreme, smuggling was still an upwardly mobile occupation within sight of the first blast furnaces, and speed trials to break world records were held on Saltburn 'flats' while collier brig construction continued within Whitby's 'haven under the hill'. Some of these long-past, and not-so-long-past, activities (ironstone mining ceased at North Skelton as recently as 1964) help to make Cleveland and North Yorkshire most fascinating subjects for this sort of 'time travel' study (but also frustrating in having to stick to a fixed transport theme!).

At Scarborough the now well-known LNER posters haunted revisitings, while along the south bank of the Tees the evocative 1960s 'shades of grey' style of photography of Colin Gifford and Malcolm Dunnett accentuated the now vast void in our current manufacturing ability - as well, of course, as the cleaner environment! A journey from, say, Middlesbrough

THE CHANGING FACE OF TEES-SIDE is demonstrated by this distant view of Newport engine shed and marshalling yard. Classified 51B under BR, the shed closed in June 1958 as a result of the opening of the nearby Thornaby depot.

The scene in 1991 shows the shed cleared and the more modern Tees marshalling yard covering the area. The only common theme between the two scenes is the Newport Vertical Lift Bridge in the centre, while road traffic in the shape of the A19 flyover now dominates the scene. A Class '08' shunter trundles past with an empty Freightliner wagon. *J. W. Armstrong Trust/Alan R. Thompson*

to Redcar today still serves to give a last glimpse of a way of life that was once so common in the Iron North, for the section between South Bank and British Steel continues to give a superb vignette of the fire and brimstone world that built the British Empire; whereupon making an exit from this 'dark tubular tunnel', the entry (and contrast) into genteel Redcar is quite a culture shock!

Journeys along such rail corridors sharply focus the subtle and mysterious passage in time, which although occurring almost imperceptibly is, even as we read, gathering momentum to make each 'yesterday' a part of a developing 'trend' that, when looked at from over our shoulders, surprises even those in Helmsley, who maintain that 'nothing ever happens here'! Only time makes the gap significant and, for their pains in identifying trends early, marketing managers are often paid disproportionate fees just to tell us how we should behave (and respond) to fit in tomorrow!

Perhaps this is a perverse sort of description of what may be considered 'just' a book of railway pictures, but none of the books in the series has been about 'just' railways! For the discerning observer the peripheral scene, especially around stations, says so much more. It is here that we see a complete cross-section of life at the time, via social habits, costume, materials in use, architecture; all joining forces to shape the world as we know it now.

In our case the railway theme was an excellent vehicle for recording not only the main but also the peripheral change because, happily, so many photographers were drawn to point their cameras only vaguely at trains, for which we are especially grateful today. This is borne out by the fact that local and general historians rely more than ever on the work of someone like John Armstrong, as he showed particular stamina in maintaining a record of changes over more than 40 years that embraced great latitude.

Level crossings seemed to have been his forte, and are especially rich for showing 'side-show' details. His camera caught an old half-cab bus at Northallerton *en route* for Ripon, and a then common tandem cycle at the gates at Potto. Even more remarkable from today's stance on safety is the unprotected open-top tractor delayed by the gates at Picton - then totally acceptable on a public highway (but, of course, 60 mph then was 'pushing it'!).

A new theme for us was finding the signalman at both Malton and Scarborough 'present' was featured at Rillington 'past' - but perhaps we'll leave that book subject for someone else!

A salutary tale for navigators concerned our trip to the Whitby area. The navigator in this case spent most of the 80-mile journey head down in old and new maps of the area. Upon arrival at Whitby a slight feeling of nausea had begun and continued to develop nicely until at the West Cliffs location his complexion was definitely becoming 'ashen'.

Keeping a brave face he approached a contractor's workman in the old station yard.

'How do? Could we have permission to take some pictures of the old station as exact copies of these old views we have here?'

'Sure. Those look interesting. There's been a few changes since. . .'

'Excuse me a moment,' said the navigator, and disappeared hurriedly behind a nearby bush, hand over mouth.

Upon reappearing, the conversation continued where it had left off. The workman never turned a hair, but simply pointed to the spot from which he thought the picture should be taken.

Another encounter provided a close shave for Alan at a remote clifftop site near Boulby mine on the Cleveland coast. He had congratulated himself upon finding the farm track that led to the coastal location, had left the car and had arrived at the rail side when a gentleman appeared and told him quite clearly to go away. This is private land, he said, and you BR people (reference to the yellow jacket perhaps) are not welcome with all the damage you've done to my perimeter fences over the years, etc, etc.

Alan though about this and decided that some 'bargaining' was necessary. He quickly produced the 'past' photo, saying 'Thought you might be interested in a picture of the old homestead. . .'

This approach stopped the other in his tracks, and in a very short time it turned out that he was none other than the local expert on railway photographic positions, and even offered to take the shot. Alan somehow convinced him that the camera was complex to work, and in a short time the Boulby load came up behind a pair of Class '20s'.

As Alan bade his host farewell, his two sons appeared from behind a hedge and asked 'Pa' if everything was all right. Alan felt their darkening shadow fall across the landscape like a large threatening cloud. He looked up and saw the two 'boys', both resembling prop forwards in an All Blacks line-out. His life briefly flashed before him; there but for the grace of God might have been his last journey - seawards!

The moral of this story is always be nice to gentlemen farmers.

One shot that almost never happened was at Easingwold, where there were problems in locating the site of the one-engine shed, now almost completely lost beneath the vegetation that had grown up since 1957. It took two visits and a total of approximately 240 miles to get this one 'in the bag'. Alan had been on the verge of aborting it (although very few if any went down as 'lost in the jungle') when he tripped over some bricks. Investigating them closely he realised that they bore a resemblance to the type of brick that could have been used in the shed construction. Much scraping along approximate perimeter foundations showed, to his disbelief, just what had become of this once populated and well-visited shed with all its amenities.

It is at places such as this that you can feel a great sadness when you consider how the railway's managers must have worried away quite a few nights dreaming up schemes to keep their tiny empire viable. They must have realised that its 'vinegar and brown paper' sort of existence could not sustain it much longer.

When you stand silently surveying a scene of past human activity, with hopeful faces full of optimism for their own future, and then compare it with the desolation and decay around you, it is a humbling experience. It makes you think that perhaps the human aspects of life - not just the bricks and mortar - deserve more attention.

An area of contrasts, then - the site of the world's first passenger-carrying railway terminus against a backdrop of Europe's largest petro-chemical plant, contrasted with Rosedale's inhospitable table-top railway and the not so very distant sylvan setting found at Pockley Gates, in beautiful Ryedale's lush vale. There can then be little doubt that 'contradiction' very suitably describes the area covered by the book.

SOUTH EAST SCOTLAND

Keith Sanders & Douglas Hodgins

In common with most areas of Britain, the railways of South East Scotland have seen much change over the last 30 years, with some lines being upgraded and incorporating all the latest technological innovations whilst others have been completely eradicated. The area was not over-endowed with lines, with very little duplication. Most of the routes were part of the North British Railway, with the Caledonian Railway being limited to providing routes from the west to Peebles, Edinburgh and Leith, and Stirling and Perth.

Many of the line closures were as a result of the run-down of the coal industry; Fife, Clackmannan and West Lothian were the main areas to suffer. However, the saddest part of the book must be the Waverley Route. This once proud line, which scaled two summits while twisting its way through the Borders, was a lifeline to towns such as Galashiels and Hawick. If the line existed today it would be an ideal candidate for treatment similar to that given to the Settle-Carlisle line. There has been very little development on the Waverley Route trackbed and mile upon mile remains just as it was when the track was lifted - even the ballast is still there. The only trackbed developments have been in the towns such as the Leisure Centre in Hawick or a new section of road in Galashiels.

The former Caledonian Railway line into Edinburgh Princes Street station has also succumbed to the motor vehicle as it is now the Western Approach Road. Elsewhere in Edinburgh and Leith the old trackbeds have been turned into a veritable maze of footpaths and cycle tracks.

Not all the old splendour has disappeared, however, for Stirling is currently a positive oasis with its many fine semaphore signals operated from a manual signal box. Regrettably these cannot really last too much longer.

THE WAY FORWARD: At first glance virtually nothing of significance seems to have changed in these two views of the station at Inverkeithing, Fife, but in the intervening 15 years much has happened. In June 1975 Birmingham RCW Class '27' works a train of track panels. All members of this Class are now withdrawn from BR service, although a number have been privately preserved.

On 3 April 1990 Brush Class '47' No 47715 *Haymarket* pulls away with the 08.40 Edinburgh-Aberdeen service. But even this 'present' picture has been overtaken by events; in 1994 this train would be comprised of Class '158' 'Sprinter' units. Inverkeithing is a commuter station for people working in Edinburgh, and a car park has been constructed accordingly. Taking a train over the Forth railway bridge is infinitely quicker than taking a car over the equivalent road bridge, especially in the rush hour. *David A. Anderson/Keith Sanders*

At the other extreme, the East Coast Main Line is now electrified with 140 mph expresses increasingly the norm. Even in the heady days of the 'A4s' or the 'Deltics', whoever would have imagined scheduled trains between Edinburgh and London taking less than 4 hours! At the time that the book was being prepared the Edinburgh-Carstairs line was being electrified, and as a result the overhead wires now pass through Princes Street Gardens. This classic location for railway photographs has been altered for ever - how the old order changes.

But at least there the railway thrives in its new form. In so many places little trace remains of former railway activity.

The overall impression I got from taking the 'present' pictures was that the Scottish sapling was alive and well, and growing exactly where I needed to stand!

While looking for the site of the old station at Elie, on the Fife coast, I was driving along a street adjacent to the railway. As there was not much sign of the former site, I politely inquired of a lady walking down the street.

'I'm not quite sure,' she said, 'but my husband will know. I will get him for you - I live just here.'

A couple of minutes later a chap came out of the house, got into my car and promptly started giving directions. After a short drive round the housing estate he told me to pull up by some new houses. He got out and started to walk across a field - I followed. He suddenly stopped in the middle of the field and said 'This is it!' The scene had changed completely, but he was right of course. After this I offered to drive him home, but he said he would walk, as the exercise would do him good.

While wandering around the old terminus station site at Leslie, also in Fife, looking for the exact spot of the 'past' picture, an old gentleman and his dog appeared. We greeted each other, and he asked me what on earth there was to photograph there, so I showed him the old photo. It turned out that he used to work at the station, and promptly started to tell me how the engine used to run round its train.

The stock would be propelled out of the station on to the viaduct, then the loco would be uncoupled and run forward into a siding. The Guard would then release the brake on the train and it would roll from the viaduct back into the station. Unfortunately the Guard was not always a good judge of braking distances, and the stock often hit the stop blocks. On one occasion it went straight through and demolished the station delivery van parked in the yard!

'The past is a foreign country,' said L. P. Hartley in the Prologue to *The Go-Between*. 'They do things differently there.'

INDEX OF LOCATIONS

'British Railways Past and Present' Nos 1-20

This index contains a complete list of all the locations featured in the first 20 volumes of the 'British Railways Past and Present' series. The location name is followed by its post-1974 county, the volume number and page number.

Thus 'past and present' photographs of Abbey in Norfolk will be found on page 16 of No 12.

The names and numbers of the 20 volumes are as follows:

* The two London books are available in a combined volume

Some volumes contain scenes from more than one county. The index of counties by volume is as follows (but please note that only part of the county may be featured in each):

The intention is that the series will eventually cover the whole country - counties and locations not found in this index will be covered by future volumes. Check the railway press for details, or send your name and address to the address on page 4 for a copy of the Past & Present complete catalogue, updated regularly.